W9-AYR-836

RACE
CARS

TOUGH WHEELS

Alain Chirinian

JULIAN MESSNER

An Important Notice for the Reader

You are not allowed by law to operate a car or a motorcycle without a driver's license. The laws of your state or country will tell you how old you must be and what tests you must pass in order to get a license to drive. In the meantime, you can enjoy reading about race cars in this book. These cars are made for driving on special tracks and roads, not on city streets.

The information in this book is based on the author's research and information received from the manufacturers of some of the cars. The specifications for the cars are general and may not apply to every car and every model that appears in the book.

Published by Julian Messner, a division of
Silver Burdett Press, Inc., Simon & Schuster, Inc.,
Prentice Hall Bldg., Englewood Cliffs, NJ 07632.

JULIAN MESSNER and colophon are trademarks of
Simon & Schuster, Inc.
Manufactured in the United States of America.

(Lib. ed.) 10 9 8 7 6 5 4 3 2 1
(Paper ed.) 10 9 8 7 6 5 4 3 2 1

Library of Congress Cataloging-in-Publication Data

Chirinian, Alain.
Race cars / Alain Chirinian.
p. cm. — (Tough wheels)
Summary: Describes fourteen of the fastest race cars in the world and how it feels to drive them.
ISBN 0-671-68030-7 (lib. bdg.); ISBN 0-671-68035-8 (pbk.)
1. Automobiles, Racing—Juvenile literature. [1. Automobiles, Racing.] I. Title. II. Series: Chirinian, Alain. Tough wheels.
TL236.C346 1989
629.2'28—dc19 88-38354
CIP
AC

Photo Credits and Acknowledgments

Pages 6 and 9 courtesy of Oldsmobile Division, General Motors Corporation
Pages 13, 14, 17, 18, 21, 26, and 29 courtesy of The Goodyear Tire and Rubber Company
Pages 58 and 61 from Centerline Photography courtesy of General Tire
Pages 42 and 45 by Wray Langston courtesy of General Tire
Pages 10 and 30 courtesy of SCCA Pro Racing
Page 22 by Sidell Tighlman courtesy of Saab
Page 25 illustrated by R. Von Sauers courtesy of Saab
Pages 33, 34, and 37 by Jeffrey R. Zwart
Pages 38 and 41 courtesy of Pontiac Motor Division, General Motors Corporation
Pages 46 and 49 by Dennis Ashlock/Nissan Motor Corporation
Pages 50 and 53 courtesy of Chevrolet Motor Division, General Motors Corporation
Pages 54 and 57 by Tom Wilson of Saleen Autosport

TABLE OF CONTENTS

OLDSMOBILE AEROTECH

PERFORMANCE:
Maximum Speed: 260+ MPH

SPECIFICATIONS

ENGINE:

Type: Four cylinder, turbocharged
Valve Gear: Dual overhead camshafts, four valves per cylinder
Displacement: 2.0 liters
Horsepower: 750

CHASSIS:

Frame: Welded tube
Front Suspension: Upper and lower wishbone
Rear Suspension: Upper and lower wishbone
Front Brakes: Ventilated disc
Rear Brakes: Ventilated disc

World's Fastest

Race cars are made for one thing: competition! It doesn't matter whether it's against another car, a clock, or a world speed record—race cars are built to push both driver and machine to the limits of speed and endurance.

Oldsmobile's Aerotech is one of the most awesome beasts ever built on four wheels. Its slick body and turbocharged engine helped it achieve an incredible speed of 218 miles per hour on its first try! Oldsmobile got champion race driver A. J. Foyt to drive the Aerotech, and there was no doubt that they would be the fastest car and driver ever on a racecourse.

Super Heavy-Duty Quad 4

The engine in the Aerotech is one of the most advanced designs ever from General Motors. It is based on the Quad 4 16-valve engine that you can buy at an Oldsmobile dealer! Added to the already powerful four-cylinder Quad 4 are dual turbochargers and intercoolers, pumping up the Aerotech's engine to 750 horsepower!

Inside the Aerotech

Sit in the narrow Aerotech cockpit, and you'll see it is much like a jet fighter. You sit beneath a plastic "bubble" right behind the front wheels. There is barely room for you to turn the steering wheel. The Aerotech circles around the track, faster and faster on each lap. You approach the banking on the oval track and shoot down the other side. You're flying in the Oldsmobile Aerotech!

AUDI 200 QUATTRO TRANS AM RACER

PERFORMANCE:
Maximum Speed: 160 MPH

SPECIFICATIONS

ENGINE:

Type: Five cylinder, turbocharged
Valve Gear: Single overhead camshaft, two valves per cylinder
Displacement: 2.1 liters
Horsepower: 510 at 7500 RPM

CHASSIS:

Frame: Unit steel
Front Suspension: Independent, strut-type
Rear Suspension: Independent, twist beam axle
Front Brakes: Ventilated disc
Rear Brakes: Ventilated disc

Championship Winner

The Trans Am racing circuit is one of the most exciting types of racing to watch. Almost all kinds of cars compete together on the same track, from V-8 engined Corvettes and Camaros to turbocharged five-cylinder Audis. The championship winner in 1988 was the four-wheel-drive, turbocharged Audi 200 Quattro.

Five-Cylinder Engine

The only five-cylinder cars on the Trans Am circuit are the Audi 200 turbo Quattros. These incredible German machines have dominated Trans Am racing since they began to race in this class. Audi used its knowledge gained from years of rally championships to help beat all the competition.

Four-Wheel Drive

Four-wheel drive has been an Audi specialty for many years. Audi builds some of the best passenger cars in the world using this system. It allows the engine to turn all four wheels of the car, automatically adjusting the balance between each wheel for incredible handling!

Rules Change

In the middle of the 1988 racing season, racing officials decided that the 200 Quattros were winning too many races. To help give the other cars in the Trans Am circuit a chance to win, race officials told Audi it would have to use smaller tires and less horsepower from the five-cylinder engine.

Trans Am Title

Even with the smaller tires and fewer horsepower, Audi kept on winning! Driven by rally champions who have great experience with four-wheel drive, the Quattros outhandled the competition and clinched the Trans Am title. Trans Am racing will always be one of the most exciting forms of racing to watch!

INDYCAR RACER

PERFORMANCE:
Maximum Speed: 220 MPH

SPECIFICATIONS

ENGINE:

Type: V-8, turbocharged
Valve Gear: Dual overhead camshafts, four valves per cylinder
Displacement: 2.6 liters
Horsepower: 700

CHASSIS:

Frame: Welded tubes, carbon fiber, and Kevlar
Front Suspension: Upper and lower wishbones
Rear Suspension: Upper and lower wishbones
Tires: Goodyear Racing
Front Brakes: Ventilated disc
Rear Brakes: Ventilated disc

Flashing by at 200 MPH

One of the most popular forms of racing to watch is Indycar racing. Once you've heard those screaming engines rush by at almost 200 miles per hour, you have to keep watching! In the grandstand, you see the bright-colored cars flash by, and you cheer each time your favorite passes!

Different Cars

Even though the cars may look the same except for the paint job, there are many different engine and chassis builders involved in Indycar racing. Each one tries to build a car that is tough enough to go the distance, can handle and brake better than the rest, and gets good gas mileage! Did we mention horsepower? Some of these cars put out over 700!

V-8 Engines

Most of the Indycars use turbocharged V-8 engines. Some teams choose to use a non-turbo V-8, which is allowed to be much larger than the smaller turbo engines. Most of the teams use engines from different manufacturers, from Porsche to Chevrolet! The chassis are also from different companies, and each team tunes its engine and chassis together to come up with a winning combination!

The Pit Stop

The pit crew is just as important to winning as the driver is. Each time the driver comes in, the pit crew members have to know exactly what to do, and to do it fast! There isn't any time to waste when an Indycar needs to make a pit stop and the other cars are still on the track!

Up Close

Look closely at an Indycar and you'll see some of the parts that help make these cars some of the fastest on any track. Huge sticky tires bite the road. Spoilers help the car "hug" the pavement at airplane-like speeds. These pieces, and many more, make Indy racing a winner every time.

IROC-Z CAMARO

PERFORMANCE:

Maximum Speed: 160 MPH

SPECIFICATIONS

ENGINE:

Type: V-8
Valve Gear: Overhead valves per cylinder
Displacement: 5.7 liters
Horsepower: 450 at 6500 RPM

CHASSIS:

Frame: Welded steel tubes
Front Suspension: Independent
Rear Suspension: Solid axle
Front Brakes: Ventilated disc
Rear Brakes: Ventilated disc

Everybody Races

When racing organizers decided to create a new racing class in which all the different racers would compete together, the International Race of Champions was born. Race car drivers from all classes, from stock cars to Indycars, were invited to compete against each other in Chevrolet Camaro IROC-Zs. The fans loved it! Seeing your favorite drivers from different race classes all together on one track is one of the best parts of IROC racing.

The Same Cars

Each Camaro in an IROC race is specially made to be exactly the same as the others. The drivers are more evenly matched, with no car being faster and giving someone a better chance at winning. This way, racing fans get a chance to see some real close competition!

No Passenger Seats

The IROC Camaros that race in this series look much like the ones you can buy at your Chevrolet dealer. But up close, the racing IROC-Zs are very different from the street models. Each body is made of fiberglass instead of steel. The doors don't open—you have to climb in through the window! Inside the IROC-Z is where you can really tell the difference between the racer and the street car. There are no passenger seats!

Better Brakes and Suspension

The Racing IROC-Z Camaros also have high-performance parts that the street cars are missing. A super heavy-duty transmission has four forward gears. Huge disc brakes are attached to each corner of the car. And special wheels and tires help the cars grip the track.

350 V-8 Engine

The engines in the IROC racers are huge, 350-cubic-inch V-8s. This is the same size engine you can buy in a street Camaro IROC-Z, but not with 450 horsepower! The street IROC-Z has about 220 horsepower, and it is one of the fastest cars around. With 450 horsepower connected to the gas pedal, IROC-Z racers make for an incredible race!

BARBER SAAB PRO SERIES

PERFORMANCE:
Maximum Speed: 165 MPH

SPECIFICATIONS

ENGINE:

Type: Four cylinder, turbocharged
Valve Gear: Dual overhead camshafts, four valves per cylinder
Displacement: 2.0 liters
Horsepower: 225 at 6000 RPM

CHASSIS:

Frame: Tubular steel
Front Suspension: Independent, wishbone
Rear Suspension: Independent, wishbone
Front Brakes: Ventilated discs
Rear Brakes: Ventilated discs

A True Racing Machine

The race begins, and you cheer as the turbo-charged 16-valve engines of the Barber Saab racers rush by you like the fastest Indycars. It's not hard to believe that each one packs 225 horse-power! Add the light weight of a 2.0-liter, four-cylinder engine to a compact chassis, and you come up with a 165-miles-per-hour racing machine!

Driving Your Best

The Barber Saab racing series was created to help people race without spending a lot of money. Racing can be a very expensive sport to compete in—some racing series might cost a million dollars to race in! But you can race a Barber Saab for a lot less money, and concentrate on driving your best.

High-Technology Engine

The engine inside the Barber Saab racers is the same one that many Saab street cars use. It is small, only 2.0 liters, but packs a lot of punch. With a turbocharger, four valves per cylinder, and an electronic "brain," the engine reaches 225 horsepower at 6000 RPM!

Highest-Quality Racing Parts

The Barber Saab racers are made of the highest-quality racing parts. Each car has a set of racing disc brakes at all four wheels. There is a very light, but strong, tubular frame. The driver can adjust the brakes from inside the car! The double shocks are also adjustable and help the car deal with bumps on the racecourse.

A Closer Look

Sit in the driver's seat of the Barber Saab racer and you notice the racing harness that straps the driver in snugly. The tiny steering wheel sits in front of a huge tachometer on the instrument panel. Starting the engine lets out a loud bark from the exhaust. You feel ready to take on the competition in your Barber Saab!

NASCAR STOCK CAR RACER

PERFORMANCE:

Maximum Speed: 200 MPH

SPECIFICATIONS

ENGINE:

Type: V-8
Valve Gear: Overhead valves, pushrod operated
Displacement: 5.9 liters
Horsepower: 500

CHASSIS:

Frame: Tubular steel
Front Suspension: Independent
Rear Suspension: Independent
Tires: Goodyear Racing
Front Brakes: Ventilated discs
Rear Brakes: Ventilated discs

Thundering V-8s

Nothing can ever match the sound and feel of a squadron of NASCAR racers going by you. The thundering V-8 engines shake the ground as they fly past each other. Each driver uses incredible driving skill and a finely tuned machine to try to reach a NASCAR championship.

NASCAR

NASCAR stands for National Association of Stock Car Auto Racing, the organization that holds stock car races. These cars are all American, all V-8 powered, and definitely not "stock," meaning they are highly modified. You can usually recognize familiar names under that bright paint job. Chevrolet, Ford, Lincoln, Mercury, Oldsmobile, and Pontiac models all compete in NASCAR racing.

Oval Tracks

Most NASCAR races are held on oval-shaped tracks, with turns in only one direction. The cars barrel through the turns at speeds of up to 200 miles per hour, rising high on the banking and then dropping down to the straightaways.

The Pit Stop

Stock cars use up a lot of fuel and wear out their tires quickly. It's very important that the pit crew be ready to change the tires and add fuel as soon as the car comes in, and send it back out on the track right away. Suddenly, a car comes in and the pit crew goes to work! Jack up the car, put on a new set of tires. Quick! Clean the windshield, pump in some fuel, and off it goes—from zero to 200 miles per hour!

BOSCH VW SUPERVEE

PERFORMANCE:
Maximum Speed: 160 MPH

SPECIFICATIONS

ENGINE:

Type: Four cylinder
Valve Gear: Single overhead camshaft, two valves per cylinder
Displacement: 1.6 liters
Horsepower: 160

CHASSIS:

Frame: Tubular steel
Front Suspension: Independent, wishbone
Rear Suspension: Independent, wishbone
Front Brakes: Ventilated discs
Rear Brakes: Ventilated discs

An Original

Supervee racing is one of the original "inexpensive" ways to go racing. Today, Supervee racing is one of the best ways to get experience and move up to some of the more expensive racing machinery. The cars are not identical to each other, as in some other classes, but the engines are all Volkswagen four cylinders. This makes for some very exciting racing!

A Pure Race Car

The incredible Supervee cars have front and rear "wings," a highly modified four-cylinder engine, and a pure racing chassis for awesome performance around the racetrack. Each manufacturer builds the fastest possible car, and each driver does his best to get to the front of the pack and stay there!

A Closer Look

On the nose of any Supervee, a "VW" is painted proudly. Next to that is the adjustable front "wing," used to keep the front end of the car glued to the ground at high speeds. Farther back are the two radiators. They are out in the open air so that the engine temperature can be kept under control. In the rear, a huge "wing" stands up behind the driver. This wing uses the rushing air to push the rear end of the car down at high speeds—up to 145 miles per hour!

Gumball Tires

To keep the Supervee from sliding off the course, special racing "slicks" are used. These tires are like gum on the street, they stick so well! Even so, driving a Supervee is difficult and takes years of training. There is a lot to learn before racing a Supervee!

On the Track

Squeeze into the cockpit of the Supervee racer and you are amazed at how close the ground is. You are only a few inches off of the track! Tiny mirrors give you a good view of what is behind you. Fire up the engine and stick the stubby gear lever into first. You blast off to Supervee competition!

FORMULA ONE RACER

PERFORMANCE:

Maximum Speed: 190 MPH

SPECIFICATIONS

ENGINE:

Type: Six and eight cylinders, most turbocharged
Valve Gear: Dual overhead camshafts, four valves per cylinder
Displacement: 1.5 to 3.5 liters
Horsepower: Up to 1000

CHASSIS:

Frame: Carbon fiber, aluminum, and Kevlar
Front Suspension: Independent, dual A-arms
Rear Suspension: Independent, dual A-arms
Front Brakes: Ventilated discs
Rear Brakes: Ventilated discs

Most Expensive

Formula One racing cars use some of the most advanced technology available anywhere today. They are also some of the most expensive cars in all of racing—often over a million dollars! Racing fans from all over the world are awed by the high speeds and skill of the drivers in this very special racing class.

Turbocharged Engines

Formula One cars use many different kinds of engines. Most are turbocharged, with four, six, or eight cylinders. Some put out as much as 900 horsepower! For the 1989 season, turbochargers will no longer be allowed in Formula One competition. Some of the teams will be using engines with even more cylinders, such as V-10 or even V-12 engines!

Expensive Materials

Some of the materials used to build Formula One cars are usually used in military aircraft. Special materials like titanium, magnesium, and aluminum are used for engine and suspension pieces. Even more advanced materials like carbon fiber are now being used—all with the goal of light weight and strength in mind. It's no wonder these cars are so expensive!

Computerized Cars

Formula One cars use lots of electronics. A computer inside the engine regulates the fuel system. Computers also send information to the pit crew to let them know everything about the engine, such as temperature and gas mileage.

A Closer Look

From far away, a Formula One car looks much like a Supervee or Barber Saab Racer. But get closer and you'll see that the Formula One car is much bigger. It is wider and longer. It has larger wheels and tires and a much more powerful engine. If you can handle one of these difficult-to-drive machines, you can push it up to almost 200 miles per hour!

TOP FUEL FUNNY CAR

PERFORMANCE:
Maximum Speed: 275 MPH in 1/4 mile

SPECIFICATIONS

ENGINE:
Type: V-8, supercharged
Valve Gear: Overhead camshaft and overhead valve designs
Displacement: 5.0 to 7.0 liters
Horsepower: 2000+

CHASSIS:
Frame: Tubular space-frame
Front Suspension: Independent, A-arms
Rear Suspension: Solid axle
Front Brakes: Discs
Rear Brakes: Discs with auxiliary parachute

Funny Cars

The monster top fuel drag racers are unlike any other type of car. They are made for one thing—to go in a short, straight line as fast as possible! Even though many have the same names as street cars, these machines are so strange-looking, they are called "funny" cars!

Like a Million Firecrackers

If you ever hear a funny car engine up close, your ears will never forgive you. There is probably no louder engine, except maybe one from a jet aircraft. The sound rattles the air around you—it's like a million firecrackers going off at once! When you go to see one of these monster motor showdowns, be sure to bring a pair of earplugs!

Huge Rear Tires

"Funnies" have very large rear tires for one reason: to keep the car moving forward instead of spinning the tires. A racer wants to spin the tires as little as possible during a race, because it wastes horsepower. These cars use small front tires because they weigh less and cut through the air better. More rubber on the ground is just not needed at the front of a Funny Car, since they only go in a straight line.

Burnouts

You'll notice that drag racers do a "burnout" before a race: they spin the rear tires in a cloud of smoke, heating them up for the best traction when starting off the line. Funny Cars also have a "wheelie bar" on the back to keep the car from flipping over on its back if the front end pulls up too high when starting. Also important is the parachute that is released after every race. This helps slow the car down better than the brakes alone can do.

CLASS 4 OFF-ROAD TRUCK

PERFORMANCE:

Maximum Speed: Ranges from 100 to 130 MPH

SPECIFICATIONS

ENGINE:

Type: Four, six, and eight cylinder types, depending on class
Valve Gear: Overhead camshaft and overhead valve designs
Displacement: Ranges from 1.8 to 5.7 liters
Horsepower: Ranges from 90 to 250

CHASSIS:

Frame: Ranges from stock unibody to steel tube
Front Suspension: Independent, multiple shock absorbers
Rear Suspension: Solid axle, multiple shock absorbers
Tires: General Tire Grabber MT
Front Brakes: Disc
Rear Brakes: Both disc and drum designs

Beating the Racecourse

Off-roading is a special kind of racing. It is more than pitting one vehicle against another, or one driver against another. The racecourse itself must be conquered before a racer even thinks about beating his competitors.

Changing Track

In other forms of racing, competitors practice on the track and then "set up" their cars for the fastest possible speed. In off-road racing, the track is always changing! The more cars that drive on it, the more it changes. Sand dunes shrink in size. Clean dirt roads become mud bogs. And sometimes the road wears out completely!

Long-Travel Suspension

There are many types of off-road vehicles, each in a different class. Trucks, cars, and motorcyles often compete on the same track. But they all have some things in common: Long-travel suspensions help absorb the shock from jumps at high speeds. Dust filters clean the air that gets into the engine. Heavy-duty shock absorbers, modified engines and braking systems—all are part of the off-road racing world.

Driving the Off-Road Racer

The fastest off-road racers usually have four-wheel drive, helping them with traction on dirt and mud. The first thing you notice is how much you get bounced around inside the truck! On the straightaways, the truck can get going quite fast, well over 100 miles per hour on some courses! At the same time, you see other racers' broken-down cars all over the course. There is no doubt that off-road racing is tough on both racer and race car!

NISSAN GTP ZX-TURBO

PERFORMANCE:
Maximum Speed: 180 MPH

SPECIFICATIONS

ENGINE:

Type: Ranges from rotary engines to six, eight, and twelve cylinders, many turbocharged
Valve Gear: Most with dual overhead camshafts, four valves per cylinder
Displacement: 1.3 to 6.5 liters
Horsepower: Up to 800

CHASSIS:

Frame: Most are tubular space-frame design
Front Suspension: Independent, upper and lower wishbone
Rear Suspension: Independent, upper and lower wishbone
Front Brakes: Ventilated discs
Rear Brakes: Ventilated discs

Grand Touring Prototype

GTP cars are some of the most competitive in all of racing. That makes it very exciting to watch these huge race cars charge up and down the track at speeds that are almost impossible to imagine. Each time you think a car is going too fast for a turn, it just pulls right through and keeps on going!

24-Hour Endurance

These cars are also used for endurance races, such as the 24 hours at Le Mans in France. In this case, the cars battle together for a full 24 hours, day and night! There is probably nothing as exciting as seeing the powerful headlights of these machines rush by at night. Racers take turns driving the car, but none get any sleep. The GTP cars make anything seem possible.

Many Competitors

Many companies build engines for the GTP racers. They use racing as a way to improve their street cars. Porsche, Jaguar, Nissan, and many others compete in GTP racing. Each company hopes to win the championship, showing people that if it can build a winning race car, it can build a great street car.

A Legend

The Nissan GTP-ZX turbo is a legend in the GTP class. Its first year out, the car won eight races in a row! Everything about this car is there to help it go fast. A super-light body was made out of a blend of aluminum, Kevlar, and carbon fiber. A turbocharged six-cylinder engine pumps out 700 horsepower. A very complicated suspension system keeps the car on the track under all that power, and disc brakes stop the car from its top speed—200 miles per hour!

SCCA CORVETTE CHALLENGE

PERFORMANCE:
Maximum Speed: 155 MPH

SPECIFICATIONS

ENGINE:

Type: V-8
Valve Gear: Overhead valves, pushrod operated
Displacement: 5.7 liters
Horsepower: 245 at 4500 RPM

CHASSIS:

Frame: Steel with fiberglass body panels
Front Suspension: Independent, upper and lower A-arms
Rear Suspension: Independent, leaf spring
Front Brakes: Ventilated disc, anti-lock

Like No Other Class

Imagine a fleet of Chevrolet Corvettes competing together on a track. The rumbling V-8s snap and bark at each other as the drivers shift gears. You are seeing real American sports cars together in a way that is like no other class of racing. These are cars just like the ones you can buy for the street, specially prepared to be identical for some close competition.

No Modifications Allowed

Each Corvette is the same as the other in this class. There are inspectors who make sure that no one has "tweaked" (changed) any part of the car that isn't supposed to be changed. In this way, drivers compete fairly against each other.

Anti-Lock Brakes

The Corvettes have an anti-lock braking system that uses a computer to help drivers avoid mistakes when driving. For instance, if you push on the brake pedal too hard on a wet track, most race cars will "lock up" or skid the wheels. But the anti-lock computer in the Corvettes doesn't let this happen, and a driver can go faster around the track in safety.

5.7-Liter Engine

The engines in these Corvettes are the same V-8s that you can buy at your Chevrolet dealer. There are some small differences that help the cars go even faster. Each engine is assembled very slowly and carefully, using "matched" parts that help it run smoother and faster. Also, only the best engine parts are chosen out of a box of pistons, for example. Then the engine is sealed up and not allowed to be touched before the race!

SALEEN RACETRUCK

PERFORMANCE:

Maximum Speed: 100 MPH

SPECIFICATIONS

ENGINE:

Type: Four cylinder
Valve Gear: Single overhead camshaft, two valves per cylinder
Displacement: 2.2 to 2.6 liters
Horsepower: 90 to 110

CHASSIS:

Frame: Unibody
Front Suspension: Independent, A-arms
Rear Suspension: Solid axle, leaf spring
Front Brakes: Disc
Rear Brakes: Drum

Racing a Minitruck

Small trucks are very popular vehicles. So it was only natural that people would want to race them! This led to the Coors Racetruck Challenge, a road racing series especially for mini-pickup trucks. These racers are allowed slight modifications to make them go faster and handle better, and this gives the spectators some fast racing to watch!

Everyone Is Racing

Most of the minitruck manufacturers have trucks that are racing. Ford, Jeep, GMC, Mitsubishi, Nissan, Toyota, Mazda, and Isuzu all race against each other in this series. People who own minitrucks especially like to watch this series because they can see their own brand of truck win races!

Tight Corners

Many of these racers are so closely matched that they try to shove each other out of the way to pass! This isn't allowed, but sometimes it can get very tight in the corners when there is a lot of traffic. When the trucks touch each other, look out! It's going to be a spin for sure, and maybe other trucks will get involved in the fun.

Do Not Pass

One of the other illegal ways to pass another truck is by "bump drafting." Bump drafting requires two trucks, one helping the other to get ahead. This usually happens when both trucks are on the same team and it is important for at least one of them to win. The two trucks follow each other very closely, and then the one in the back "bumps" the other one into the lead! It sounds dangerous, and it is.

OFF-ROAD ULTRASTOCK COMPETITOR

PERFORMANCE:

Maximum Speed: Up to 65 MPH, depending on track conditions

SPECIFICATIONS

ENGINE:

Type: Four, six, and eight cylinders
Valve Gear: Overhead valve and overhead camshaft designs
Displacement: Any stock displacement
Horsepower: Ranges from 75 to 200+ horsepower

CHASSIS:

Frame: Stock body and frame
Front Suspension: Stock design with multiple shock absorbers
Rear Suspension: Stock design with multiple shock absorbers
Tires: General Tire XP2000 Line
Front Brakes: Disc
Rear Brakes: Disc and drum

Rough Riding

Unlike most other off-road vehicles, Ultrastock competitors are almost like the cars you can buy for the street. Ultrastock means that the racers are allowed very few modifications. Apart from their suspensions, they are mostly stock! That makes it especially hard on both the cars and the drivers—they each have to be in good shape to be able to finish a race!

Watch For Dust

One of the biggest enemies of any off-road racer is the amount of mud, and especially dust, that gets into the car. This dust can clog air filters, wear out parts faster, and blind the driver. This is why the cars that can compete successfully in the Ultrastock class are really tough wheels.

The Ultrastock Pulsar

The Nissan Pulsar is a hot little car that does very well in the Ultrastock class. Its dual overhead camshaft, 16 valve engine pumps out the horsepower, and a rugged chassis design keeps the Pulsar on the track and out of the pits. The Pulsar also uses street-legal XP2000 General Tires that allow it to take a hard bite out of the dirt road ahead!

Stadium Racing

Imagine taking a bunch of race cars and putting them indoors to race. That's exactly what happens in the Ultrastock class—the jumps, ditches and turns of the desert are brought indoors! It's an experience that no one should miss!

Start Your Racer

Start up your Ultrastock, let's race! The field seems clear ahead, and you bounce up and down in your seat. You catch up to another car, and behind him, his wheels kick up all the dust and dirt right at you! You turn the wheel slightly and stand on the gas, passing him. It's competition in the off-road Ultrastock class!

GLOSSARY

Aerotech—Oldsmobile's record-setting race car.
Anti-lock Brakes—A braking system that uses a computer to modulate the car's brakes, keeping them from locking up to maintain braking control.
Barber Saab—A class of race car using Saab engines.
"Bump Drafting"—A dangerous and illegal passing technique popular in the minitruck class. Bump drafting involves two cars, one "bumping" the other ahead of the race leader to pass.
Burnout—A technique used by drag racers to prepare the tires for a race. After driving over some chalk or water, the driver punches the accelerator for a moment, spinning the rear tires to heat them up. This allows for better acceleration during a drag race.
Chassis—A system of components that links the driver and engine to the road. The chassis includes the frame, suspension, wheels, and brakes.
Cylinder—A circular hole inside the engine in which a piston moves up and down.
Disc Brakes—A flat, round disc attached to the wheel that is "grabbed" by a caliper when the brake pedal is pushed, stopping the vehicle.
Drag Racer—A race car that is built only to travel as fast as possible in a straight line in a drag race.
Engine Electronics—Electronic controls in the engine that use a computer to precisely regulate important functions. This includes fuel delivery and ignition timing.
Fiberglass—A material made of special glass fibers that are bonded together.
Four Valves Per Cylinder—A cylinder head design that uses four valves to control intake and exhaust in the combustion chamber. This is a very common design in racing engines.
Four-Wheel Drive—A car that transmits engine power to all four wheels at once, although not always in the same amount. Most four-wheel drive systems adjust the amount of front-to-rear-wheel engine power depending on road and speed conditions.
Funny Car—A special class of drag racer that looks like a comic version of a street car. One of the fastest types of vehicles on Earth.
Indycar—A class of racing vehicle using mainly turbocharged V-8 engines, racing on oval tracks. Speeds are some of the highest of any class.

Intercooler—A device used to lower the temperature of incoming air to an engine's turbocharger, allowing racers to tune more power out of the engine.
IROC-Z—Chevrolet Camaros used to race in the International Race of Champions Series.
Long-Travel Suspension—A suspension design used mainly in off-road machines, allowing for lots of up-and-down suspension movement for incredible shock absorption.
Minitruck—A small pickup truck used in the Minitruck Challenge Series.
Off-Road—Racing off paved roads, such as in desert racing.
Piston—A circular piece of metal that moves up and down inside the cylinder. The piston is forced to move by the force of an explosion in the combustion chamber.
Pit Crew—The team of mechanics and others who work to get the race car back on the track after making a pit stop.
Pit Stop—A short stop off the track during a race for extra fuel, a tire change, or repairs to the race car.
Quad 4 Engine—Oldsmobile's newest four-cylinder engine. The record-setting Aerotech uses a version of the Quad 4.
Quattro—Audi's four-wheel-drive system. Also used to name their four-wheel-drive vehicles, as in Audi 200 Turbo Quattro.
Racing Harness—A special set of belts and straps that hold a race driver firmly in the driver's seat.
Shock Absorbers—A round tube that slides within another tube filled with special liquid and/or gas, which dampens its movement and that of the suspension.
Slicks—Special tires with no tread, used on a dry racetrack.
Stock Car—A class of car in NASCAR racing. All are stock-bodied, V-8 engined race machines.
Supervee—A class of race car using Volkswagen engines.
Suspension—The link between the wheels and the frame of the car. The suspension absorbs road shock and determines the handling characteristics of the car.
Tachometer—A gauge that reads engine speed.
Turbocharger—A small turbine that is spun at very high speeds by exhaust gases. The turbocharger forces extra air and fuel into the engine, allowing a smaller engine to have as much horsepower as a much larger engine.
Wheelie Bar—A small set of extra wheels on the back of a drag racer that helps to keep the car from flipping over on its back when racing.

INDEX